AMAZING MYSTERIES

HIPPOGRIFFS

BY MELISSA GISH

CREATIVE EDUCATION • CREATIVE PAPERBACKS

Published by Creative Education and Creative Paperbacks
P.O. Box 227, Mankato, Minnesota 56002
Creative Education and Creative Paperbacks are imprints of
The Creative Company
www.thecreativecompany.us

Design by The Design Lab
Production by Rachel Klimpel
Art direction by Rita Marshall
Printed in the United States of America

Photographs by Alamy (PRISMA ARCHIVO), Bridgeman Images
(Gustave Doré/Look and Learn), Creative Commons Wikimedia
(Jean-Auguste-Dominique Ingres/Art Renewal Center, Internet Ar-
chive Book Images/Flickr), Dreamstime (Patrick Guenette), Deviant
Art (bonbonka, Nele-Diel, Reptangle, Skye-Fyre, verreaux), Getty
Images (Fine Art/Corbis Historical, Orlando Sentinel/Tribune News
Service, Stuart C. Wilson/Stringer/Getty Images Entertainment),
Pixabay (Gordon Johnson, OpenClipart-Vectors), Shutterstock (Ender
BAYINDIR)

Cover and page 1 image courtesy of José Heleno de Souza Melo.

Library of Congress Cataloging-in-Publication Data
Names: Gish, Melissa, author.
Title: Hippogriffs / Melissa Gish.
Series: Amazing mysteries.
Includes bibliographical references and index.
Summary: A basic exploration of the appearance, behaviors, and
origins of hippogriffs, the part-horse, part-eagle mythological crea-
tures known for their flying. Also included is a story from folklore
about how a hippogriff helped save a prince.

Identifiers:
ISBN 978-1-64026-490-8 (hardcover)
ISBN 978-1-68277-041-2 (pbk)
ISBN 978-1-64000-617-1 (eBook)
This title has been submitted for CIP processing under LCCN
2021937596.

First Edition HC 9 8 7 6 5 4 3 2 1
First Edition PBK 9 8 7 6 5 4 3 2 1

Table of Contents

Magical Mix-Up   4

Mythic Origins   7

High Fliers   11

Celebrations   12

Beastly Relatives   19

Familiar Face   20

A Hippogriff Story   22

Read More   24

Websites   24

Index   24

The hippogriff is an animal that has the body and back legs of a horse. It has the front legs, wings, and head of an eagle. Hippogriffs can fly.

Part of the hippogriff's name comes from the Greek word for horse, hippos.

In 1516, an Italian poet wrote about snowy mountains where all kinds of monsters lived. That is where hippogriffs were born from magical eggs.

The poem that talked about hippogriffs in the 1500s is long—it has almost 40,000 lines!

The blend of horse and griffin (opposite) gives a hippogriff its features.

A hippogriff's mother is a horse. Its father is a **griffin**. Griffins sometimes eat horses. Only a powerful love can bring these enemies together. For this reason, a hippogriff is sometimes a sign of love.

griffin a creature with the body of a lion and the head and wings of an eagle

Hippogriffs stand about nine feet (2.7 m) tall. Their wings stretch 20 feet (6.1 m) across. They can fly beyond the clouds. They have sharp beaks and claws. Only magical people can train hippogriffs. These beasts are loyal to their masters.

Hippogriffs in the Harry Potter series are known for being proud.

In 28 B.C., Roman leader Caesar Augustus made a building for Apollo, god of the sun. On it was a stone hippogriff.

"Caesar" (SEE-zer) was the Roman title for some of their kings.

Hippogriffs can fly about a week after they are born.

Stories about men riding hippogriffs into battle were told for hundreds of years. Hippogriffs appear in 16th-century **epic** poetry. They serve magicians and go with knights on dangerous missions.

epic a form of poetry that tells a long story about heroes and their feats

In the 1600s, Italian kings and queens held plays and dances called masques. Men dressed as Greek gods rode machines that looked like hippogriffs. Hippogriff floats sailed in river parades.

Some Greek helmets had griffins or hippogriffs on them.

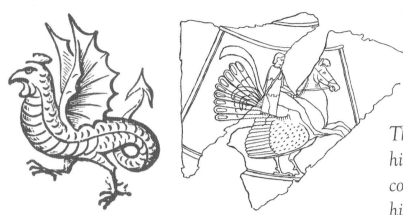

These pictures show a hieracosphinx (opposite), cockatrice (far left), and hippalectryon (left).

The cockatrice of British **folklore** is a winged dragon. It has the head of a rooster. **Ancient** Greek stories told of the hippalectryon. This is a horse with the hind legs, tail, and wings of a rooster. The Egyptian hieracosphinx is a falcon-headed lion.

ancient in the distant past and no longer in existence

folklore traditional beliefs, stories, or customs that are passed on by word of mouth

In the world of Harry Potter, 12 hippogriffs live at Hogwarts School of Witchcraft and Wizardry. Buckbeak is one of them. He becomes Harry's friend. Buckbeak's keeper is Hagrid.

Buckbeak and the other Hogwarts hippogriffs are known for their different-colored coats.

A Hippogriff Story

Long ago, an evil creature kidnapped a prince. The demon took the prince to a tall mountain far away. The king sent his knights to rescue his son, but the mountain was too high. Then a sorceress saddled her hippogriff. She rode it beyond the clouds. She put the demon to sleep. Then she carried the prince home on her hippogriff.

sorceress a woman who practices the magical arts

Read More

Kershaw, Stephen P. *Mythologica: An Encyclopedia of Gods, Monsters, and Mortals from Ancient Greece.* Minneapolis: Wide Eyed Editions, 2019.

Marsico, Katie. *Beastly Monsters from Dragons to Griffins.* Minneapolis: Lerner, 2017.

Sautter, A. J. *A Field Guide to Griffins, Unicorns, and Other Mythical Beasts.* Mankato, Minn.: Capstone, 2015.

Websites

Near Human Intelligence: All You Need to Know About the Hippogriff!
https://www.youtube.com/watch?v=WYSdkanVRP0
Learn more about hippogriffs.

Wizarding World: Pottermore's Guide to Hippogriffs
https://www.wizardingworld.com/features/pottermore-guide-to-hippogriffs
Read interesting facts about hippogriffs of Hogwarts.

Note: Every effort has been made to ensure that the websites listed above are suitable for children, that they have educational value, and that they contain no inappropriate material. However, because of the nature of the Internet, it is impossible to guarantee that these sites will remain active indefinitely or that their contents will not be altered.

Index

appearance 4, 11
eggs 7
flying 4, 11, 22
history 12, 16

masters 11, 18
parents 8
similar beasts 19
stories 15, 19, 20